Paul Revere's Ride

by Lori Mortensen
illustrated by Craig Orback

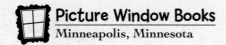
Picture Window Books
Minneapolis, Minnesota

Special thanks to our advisers for their expertise:
Susanna Robbins, M.A.
Former Assistant Editor, OAH Magazine of History
Terry Flaherty, Ph.D., Professor of English
Minnesota State University, Mankato

Editor: Jill Kalz
Designer: Abbey Fitzgerald
Page Production: Melissa Kes
Art Director: Nathan Gassman
Editorial Director: Nick Healy
Creative Director: Joe Ewest
The illustrations in this book were created with acrylic paint.

Photo Credits: cover (leather texture), Shutterstock/Leigh Prather; 2, 10–11, 12–13,
24–25, and 29 (parchment texture), Shutterstock/AGA; 29, Shutterstock/Jason Figert

Picture Window Books
151 Good Counsel Drive
P.O. Box 669
Mankato, MN 56002-0669
877-845-8392
www.picturewindowbooks.com

Printed in the United States of America.

 All books published by Picture Window Books
are manufactured with paper containing at least
10 percent post-consumer waste.

Library of Congress Cataloging-in-Publication Data
Mortensen, Lori, 1955–
Paul Revere's ride / by Lori Mortensen ; illustrated by Craig Orback.
p. cm. — (Our American story)
Includes index.
ISBN 978-1-4048-5537-3 (library binding)
1. Revere, Paul, 1735-1818—Juvenile literature. 2. Statesmen—Massachusetts—
Biography—Juvenile literature. 3. Massachusetts—Biography—Juvenile literature.
4. Massachusetts—History—Revolution, 1775-1783—Juvenile literature. I. Orback,
Craig. II. Title.
F69.R43M67 2010
973.3'311092—dc22
[B]   2009006893

Paul Revere was a silversmith. He made things out of silver. He never thought that one day he would become an American hero.

Paul lived in Boston, Massachusetts. At the time, Massachusetts was one of 13 colonies. The Colonies belonged to Great Britain.

King George III and the British government made all the rules for the Colonies. They taxed almost everything. They even taxed the Colonists' tea.

The Colonists grew unhappy with Great Britain's rules. They said they would not pay any more taxes. Dressed in disguise, the angry Colonists dumped boxes of tea into the harbor.

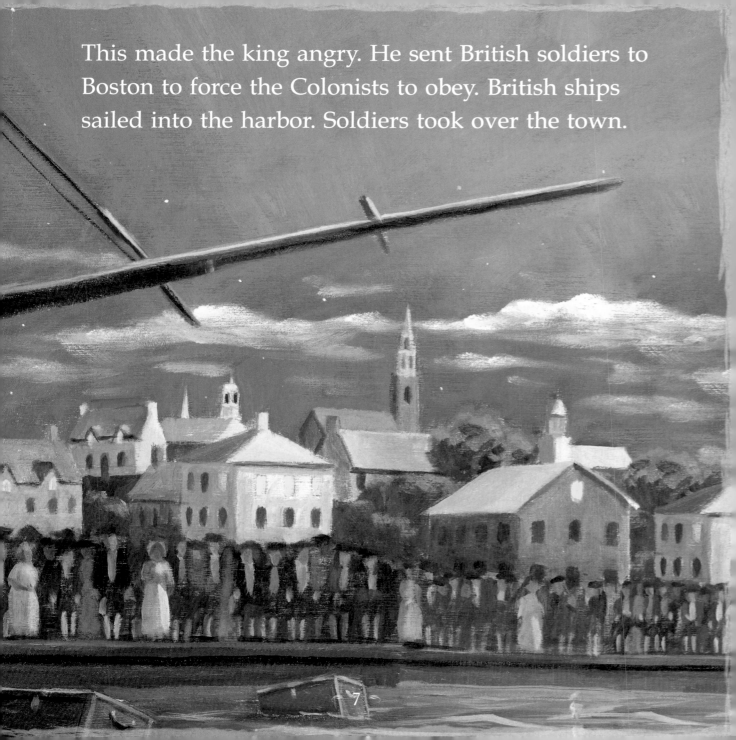

This made the king angry. He sent British soldiers to Boston to force the Colonists to obey. British ships sailed into the harbor. Soldiers took over the town.

But the king's plan did not work.

The Colonists wanted to make their own laws. They wanted America to be its own country. They decided to fight for their freedom from Great Britain.

Paul Revere joined the fight. On the night of April 18, 1775, he learned British soldiers were heading to Lexington—that night! The soldiers planned to take the Colonists' weapons and arrest their leaders.

The Colonists had to be warned. There was no time to lose. Paul said he would sound the alarm.

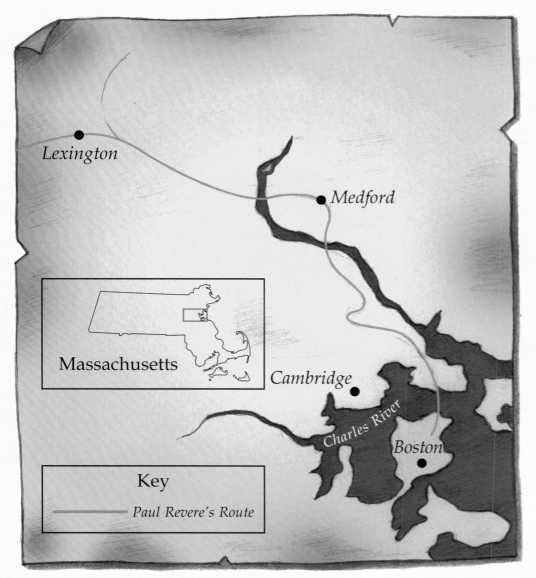

Massachusetts

Cambridge

Charles River

Boston

Lexington

Medford

Key

⸺ Paul Revere's Route

Would the British soldiers march out of Boston by land? Or would they row across the Charles River? Paul knew the answer. To send a signal to the other Colonists, he rushed to the Old North Church.

He asked his friends to hang two lanterns in the bell tower. The lanterns were an important sign. One lantern meant "by land." Two meant "by sea." British soldiers were rowing across the Charles River!

Next, Paul raced to the harbor. Two friends waited in a small boat. They tied cloth to the oars and pushed off into the water.

The cloth quieted the sound of the oars. It would not be easy getting past the British ships.

Luckily, no one saw them. When they reached the other side, Paul leaped onto a waiting horse and rode toward Lexington. The horse's name was Brown Beauty.

Suddenly, two British soldiers jumped out from behind the trees. The soldiers tried to stop Paul.

But Brown Beauty was too fast. Paul escaped through the woods.

Paul rode through the streets from town to town.
He warned everyone in his path.

The Colonial soldiers, called minutemen, quickly gathered their guns. They were ready to fight in a minute's time. When the British soldiers came, the minutemen would be waiting.

Paul reached Lexington around midnight. He then joined two other riders going to Concord.

The town of Concord held a large number of the Colonists' weapons. It would be a target for the British soldiers.

But before long, Paul and his friends were surrounded. The other two riders got away. Paul could not escape.

The soldiers held Paul and took Brown Beauty.
They asked many questions. When they heard
shots, they let Paul go and hurried away.

Paul's ride was over. He would not get far
without his horse. He walked through the
fields back to Lexington.

When the British soldiers reached Concord
in the morning, the minutemen met them.
Shots were fired. Many men died.

After a few hours, the British soldiers gave up and headed back toward Boston. The Colonists won their first battle for freedom. But they might not have won without Paul's brave ride.

Eight years later, in 1783, the Colonists won their freedom from Great Britain. The United States became its own country.

Today, visitors at the Old North Church can see a statue of Paul Revere and Brown Beauty. It honors the silversmith who became a great American hero.

Timeline

1734	Paul Revere is born in Boston, Massachusetts.
1746	Twelve-year-old Paul learns to work as a silversmith.
1773	Colonists dump boxes of tea into Boston Harbor. The event is now called the Boston Tea Party.
1775	Paul warns the Colonists on his famous ride.
1775	The Revolutionary War begins.
1781	British soldiers surrender in Yorktown, Virginia, on October 19.
1783	The United States and Great Britain sign a peace agreement. The Revolutionary War ends.

Glossary

arrest — to take to jail

colonies / Colonies — lands ruled by another country; the 13 British colonies that became the United States

colonists / Colonists — people who live in a colony; people who lived in the 13 Colonies

harbor — a safe body of water near land for ships

lantern — a metal case used for protecting light, such as a flame

minutemen — volunteer soldiers who were not part of the regular Colonial army; they were ready to fight in a minute's time

Revolutionary War — (1775–1783) the American colonies' fight against Great Britain for freedom

silversmith — someone who makes things out of silver

tax — a government fee

To Learn More

❧ More Books to Read ❧

Corey, Shana. *Paul Revere's Ride*. New York: Random House, 2004.

Longfellow, Henry Wadsworth. *Paul Revere's Ride*. Honesdale, Pa.: Boyds Mills Press, 2003.

Mara, Wil. *Paul Revere*. New York: Children's Press, 2004.

Niz, Xavier. *Paul Revere's Ride*. Mankato, Minn.: Capstone Press, 2006.

❧ Internet Sites ❧

FactHound offers a safe, fun way to find Internet sites related to this book. All of the sites on FactHound have been researched by our staff.

Here's all you do:

Visit *www.facthound.com*

FactHound will fetch the best sites for you!

Look for all of the books in the Our American Story series:

The First American Flag

President George Washington

Paul Revere's Ride

Writing the U.S. Constitution